TRUST THE DAMAGE

First published in 2024 by
The Dedalus Press
13 Moyclare Road
Baldoyle
Dublin D13 K1C2
Ireland

www.dedaluspress.com

ISBN 978-1-915629-25-8(paperback)
ISBN 978-1-915629-24-1 (hardback)

Dedalus Press titles are available in Ireland
from Argosy Books (www.argosybooks.ie) and in the UK
from Inpress Books (www.inpressbooks.co.uk)

Cover photograph by David Underland / Pexels.

The Dedalus Press receives financial assistance from
The Arts Council / An Chomhairle Ealaíon.

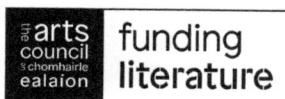

the arts council
an chomhairle ealaíon

funding
literature

TRUST THE DAMAGE

TRUDIE GORMAN

DEDALUS PRESS

Author's Note

This book was written over five years of my life, in the fragments of time I found between episodes of illness. It was written in waiting rooms at doctor surgeries, in the in-between hours of A&E visits in the middle of the night. It was written on my phone lying in bed, on the days when I didn't have the strength to sit up. It was written on late summer evenings at my desk in Dublin Fringe. It was written on bus and train journeys, and in the dead of night when the weight of sickness kept me awake. What started as a way for me to make sense of my sick experience, to understand the relationship between poverty and my health, became a method of survival and resistance. Slowly, and never in a straight line, I wrote my way back into my body. This book is testament to how, even in sickness, we bloom.

Contents

For all those whose lives have been belittled,
may your voices sing.

"How to care for the injured body, the kind of body that can't hold the content it is living? And where is the safest place when that place must be someplace other than in the body?"
—Claudia Rankine

Body,
as animal

Bless the sky that watches the same old violence

The moon watches the Gardaí pin me against
the wall again for the simple crime of walking
home alone at night.
They ask where I've been,
I tell them about the intermittent running
water on Mars.
They say I must be stupid.

I climb inside their mouths, say
hunger
and
help
and
grief
But nothing keeps.
Above me Nike Air Maxes quiver on the telephone wire
in the night breeze.

The moon tells me later how it looked from above:
that I was small and glowing, almost all teeth,
that their laughter never reached their throats.
She says, *the stars are tired of the same old show.*

I go to the station the next morning,
wait only to be asked to leave.
My mother says, *what will I do with my righteous baby?*
I say: bleed.

Instead of giving up

The nurse says the risk of infection with a catheter
is too high, so you piss in a pot beside the bed

most nights for two years.
Funny, isn't it, what we'll do for forgiveness.

Just to stay in the soft, wet home
of our quiet lives

Eventually, you grow so used to sickness,
your organs forget their old names,

and instead, answer only to the bruised sites
of your late twenties.

So that every time you sit in the lonely
of the tragic dark, your life screams.

What they really mean when they say

I'm broke too: I have the luxury of savings
We didn't have much growing up either: We only had one car
You don't look sick: You're lying
At least you're not dead: I can't help you
You're not working class anymore: Nothing stays living in the body
Have you tried meditation? It's all in your head
It's your own fault if you're still poor: I hate you
I'm so sorry: Stop crying on the bus
Your parents didn't work hard enough: Poverty is a myth
University isn't for people like you: You don't belong here
You're looking for attention: I don't care if you live or die
How bad is the pain on a scale of 1–10? There is no language for
    the body
You're scrounging off the state: You're an animal
The waiting list is five years: You don't deserve the sky
I love you: Please don't kill yourself

Echolalia

There's things when I'm like this/touch above all else will only kill me harder/voices are nails in bone/everything is fire inside/safe safe safe safe safe safe/the words between my teeth over and over/ don't touch me or I'll scream on the bus/don't look me in the eyes/I'm begging you/don't try to hug me goodbye/it's only a destiny that hurts/my body is a fire escape/ everything is an exit wound/haven't you heard/I'll run I'll run/ don't call anyone/just leave me rocking on the hard wood floor/ allow me to be an animal for a while/even if it makes you long for another girl/a good girl/bad bad bad/I just need the claws to release/can you make them stop singing/everything is a death march now/I told you before/just bring me the familiar/hang me where it hurts/stay away till it's over/don't talk in language/this is my uncaging/what's blacker than the abyss/don't blame me for how deep/I was always meant to be/feel everything in sirens/love everything bigger than sky

Home

When they say we can all make it
if we work hard, what they really mean is
  close your eyes, and you can dream
  the sky into nothingness;
the overdoses, the slow violence.

Eventually, my living turns into gloat.
Call it meritocracy, but it tastes
like sin when the funerals repeat
with the seasons and I'm still here,

slow rasping onto the window pane,
nightmaring the whole estate into
a dark mirage and growing bloody
from the make-believe.

Home is a lingering wound when
nothing grows but endings.
Streets wet with rain and time passing.
I used to think we could all get out of here,
the myth of a just world
bloomed in my chest too.

But every time another boy mistakes
violence for magic,
I can't know for sure that he's wrong.
Maybe we're all only magic-makers,
funeraling our living so that our names,
are something more than memory.

What's the opposite of horizon?
I can feel it in my throat now,

that twisted inverse,
    that soft cage.
Maybe one day, I won't miss
what hurts me most.

Routine nightmare

1

It wasn't that I wanted the emergency room again,
it was that I had crawled up the stairs three times
that night and what you call nightmare was my
strange regime.

2

The thing that left me never had a name,
just a sound that pierced through every life
I had before longing, before disease took
what it could stomach.

3

I suppose you could call it grief, what came after:
the slow howl on the bathroom floor,
how I wore black to every appointment.
The nurses talked about eating meat as if the flesh

4

of another animal had anything to do with living.
I'll remember this harder than most:
the doctor's eyes when I asked about hope,
how he looked at me like he'd seen me many times.

5

I could tell it like a story
but still it would stay;
the empty glow of smashed up vials,
the way nothing changed.

It hurts to grow towards the sky

The dinner table is bruised into silence
when your grandmother starts to talk about
all the single mothers getting houses for free.
I feel my past rise inside my body
and into my throat.

Scrounging off the state.
A hot wound in my mouth.
You squeeze my hand beneath the table,
but that's not enough for an animal
bowling towards survival.

I excuse myself.
There are two bathrooms in your house
and that's still a luxury.
In the glow of electricity
I remember the night-time outside;
dark and spreading.
I look in the mirror, take a breath,
tell my whole life to quiet down
just a little longer.

If I die from not being believed

then the joke really was on me.
My mouth loose with the years
I spent screaming for attention.

On the third month of sickness,
my legs go numb
from another night failing
to get better.

The doctor surveys my bruised
state, limp in the borrowed wheelchair,
types his notes, asks, *could it be in your head?*
I dream of his heart failing.

Three years pass and not much changes,
except how easily I forget.
The doctor takes bloods again.
Have you tried Valium?
I cut out his tongue inside my head.

I learn not to call the ambulance
in an emergency,
some things hurt harder
than dying.

The body shudders towards an ending.
I feel her peeling away from me.
The fever that last weeks only wants
to love me, so I leave.

They find me pale and unfurled
on my bedroom floor.
The autopsy results are clear:
good news, there was nothing wrong.

Later, in the congress of the operating theatre,
they harvest my skin to clothe
another sick girl
in her doomed destiny.

Years from now she'll sit across from a doctor,
shaking inside the horror of her own bad body.
Have you tried the contraceptive pill?
She'll open the portal of her mouth:
my voice will scream.

Architecture of disease

And what can you hold, if not yourself?
Other than your dark past come alive again
and your body, always your body.
Did you really not see it coming?
Everyone round here has been sick for years.
Your own mother even, her organs cut out
to preserve what was left.

> The methadone clinic in the chemist
> every Tuesday and Friday,
> children watching parents become less alive.
> How many slow deaths live inside
> what you've witnessed?

This morning your mother came home
to find you kneeling in wet grass.
You don't know how to be alone these days,
not with your old life so gone from you.

> She tells you about Mary around the corner,
> the cancer come back and gone through her.
> She tells you about the woman who lives
> on the avenue waiting for a surgeon
> to take her breast so new life can bloom.

You're used to these stories,
used even to the men who come out
of the psychiatric ward with eyes
like dead water, just a winter away
from frozen.

But somewhere along the road,
you stopped believing this was fated,
started hungering for the power
of the self-preservation.

And instead of the script of disease
your community was given
forty years ago,
you wake one day and know
that everything you can name,
has the strength to splinter open.

Body,
as time machine

Pernicious Anaemia Ward, 1931

Your breath smells like death, but I love it
Sweet home, feed me as if I was your own

I'm gagging for it
I'm dying slow

They took my bloods in the last shipment
They sent pieces of me to the queen

Don't you see?
I loved too mad

I let the damage spread
I'll watch you do it,

cut the liver of another animal,
sinew like rubber and blood with the answer

Put it inside you, lips first,
then through

Wait for the gut to make magic
of another thing's death

It could take days, I stay
I've stayed all these years

In my measured emergency,
in my darling death-bed

in my sick, sick dreams
There's a chalice for you

to heave into, you must know
they try to make it beautiful

Life-giver, I suckle
from your purge

The sweet tang of expulsion,
the detritus of you

inside me now
I feel the living rise up

The doctors say I might long for nothing
I'll walk again someday

If I make you my god,
Won't you come again?
Won't you send me skywards?

Watering my youth on the back garden shed

Midnight, and I'm licking sugar
off the dappled concrete again.
There's nowhere else to go
to dream, so I come up here.

The darkened gardens are below,
I am at home between soil and sky.
On any other night the boys next door
might be crawling the walls in their

perennial pruning of the law.
And who could blame them for trying
to win in their own evergreen way?
I have never called them crooked,

those boys and their dazzling dreams.
I yearned for blooming too.
The night is quiet now, with none
of its usual siren-answers.

It is simply my life resting in the shadow
of the estate, knowing all small futures
are watered in the certainty
of the dark.

All our bright endings/Social skills group for autistic youth

I say the right things some of the time,
but the boy is still waiting.
The room still close with all our
beautiful fumbling.

The facilitators pour orange juice
into small white-moon cups.
The boy is looking at the wall when
he tells me; it happened last spring,
he still smells her perfume when it rains.

The group stare, the one good
radiator careens. I try not to lose
myself in the familiarity of his grief.
I'm sorry, but it's not the language
we were born in.

I want to tell him it's okay
to be an animal, but time bleeds.
They made us strange, we know
this somehow and yet
we go quietly.

Later, I imagine the boy in the hook
of the night, keening through the walls.
The orange juice goes sour in the afterglow.
The room remembers.

Waiting rooms

And the next day is always a school day,
I spend it with people I'll fear years later
and people I won't.
149 days out of the mental hospital,
I bury everything one winter at a time.
I've lost a stone of my own presence
and can't hold down most things/
the colour of wine/endings.

Waiting rooms become familiar in the dark,
seasons drip into each other like
wet animals crawling home.
The doctors don't know what to do
with me/ their own crooked assumptions,
but I keep going back, wanting a way out
of my own body.

Slouching towards anything

Sometimes the darkest of affairs
 happen in the middle of the day.
The 38 bus shuttling towards home,
how that same journey ricochets through
years of so many small lives.
But there's a sudden halting –
a drunk elderly man unconscious,
a driver tired of the predictability of poverty.
The Gardaí are called, and they come
with their scathing regard,
handle him up the aisle,
toss him onto the street outside.
I'm younger than I am now,
but old enough to know:
stay quiet and small.
A stranger on the ground now,
his trousers w i l t around him.
A nappy – brief glimpse into brutal life.
One of the Gardaí spits.
The bus shudders away.
I don't cry until later that night
and when I do, the whole estate
howls out of me.

Visiting my mother on the cancer ward

The night is limp with stars when I take the train to the hospital, after the second operation to pull the sickness purring inside your body. I am nineteen which is to say I know nothing yet of the things to come; my triumphs blinking at the edges of a future. In the hospital hum you are vomiting up the anaesthetic and your sister hugs me like I'm her own and the nurse tells us this is normal, like she knows every animal chooses the better poison in end. You are smaller with yet more organs gone and it's my first day without makeup which means more than it should if I wasn't still steeped in the burden of girlhood. You sleep deeper than you have in years, and I imagine the things within you; those luminous things that live inside your blood and on your skin and behind your eyes, all of them deciding simply to stay while you dream. I close my eyes and you're not my mother anymore, you're a songbird and the sky has always said yes. Your job was never lost and the boys on our street never die with needles in their arms like arrows pointing towards god and the ambulances never siren too late. This small, winged birth is what you deserve, and it's never beaten down or sparked out and when you wake up, this is all that you'll remember; how the azure sky said stay alive stay alive and you listened in exquisite defiance of all the things you were told could never moult and

then rise.

Things I try hard to forget

Dusk, somewhere.
The staircase spanning our hurried youth.
The thump-thumping of neighbours against the wall
and all the things I cannot see.
A mouth opening,

gnarling in the slow dark

 and his words becoming the past.

Her body, getting older and wide with rage behind me.
Glass splintered on the carpet.
The sickly scent of wine seeping deeper.
Bodies becoming weapons becoming memory.
The light swelling shut.
The truth coming home.

Mad girl at the asylum

There's always lonely.
                Whatever way you cut it,

                        an animal inside a body inside the world.

There's always the mental hospital,
                how the legacy of the feeble-minded
                                lived
in every slow drug they fed you.

There's always the elderly woman who waved from her window
    every day
                at the space she imagined was freedom.
          How you waved back sometimes from the cage
outside the residents' room
                     and dreamed of the garden.

We weren't allowed outside often,
                    but once the nurses took us on a walk
           to Fairview Park and you swore you didn't imagine
the way the outside people shuddered in orbit around you,

just like in the movies,
except in real life it hurt harder to be at the periphery
                    of everyone's worst nightmare.

There's always nightmare.
                How it came for months the same way:

the nurses shaking you each night
with a torch between their teeth,

until your teenage body grew out of madness
and into every grief history left behind.

There's always history.
                    Legacy lived inside your mouth even then,
what you believed was darkness was only ever a portal opening
            and now every woman whose ever lost her mind
                                        returns
in the riot of the night to find voice
                is still sky
and how beautiful, how dangerous you are
when you sing.

Body,
as sermon

Poem in honour of Taylor Swift's birthday

It's December and people are dying,
but I get on the plane all the same,
summon the symptoms I trust.

I find another sick bed, satisfy my blood lust
with films about what it's like to be healthy
and in Paris.

My mother made me this way, all nectar
and no money. The world keeps burning,
I heard it on the news. It's okay, I'm white

so I'll be saved for last,
but I'm poor, so I keep yearning
for that sweet middle-class splendour

for just a few bony years. On the 13th,
I think of her mother, pray the cancer left her
like it did mine, imagine her soft red lips around

an aging red wine, writing the eulogy
for all that quiet hunger.
I pray to her feline figure nightly,

defend her to anyone who will listen.
I want to decant her music inside of you,
but that's too (easy).

I want you to bruise so tender it spills.
When I think too much about climate change,
I cry on first dates. It's okay, I might be poor,

but I'm still pretty.

A skyline to believe in

I'd never been more godless than that night.
It must have been summer, but not inside my body.
And I wanted you the way a knife wants a wound
to speak its own hunger.

I was already living in a funeral,
writing my own eulogy each night before sleep.
So when you asked if we could play pretend,
I made a hole out my life and let you enter.

Your hands around my neck in our dark fantasy,
my mouth a wide-open tragedy.
I was dirty, and our whole city too,
the housing crisis sick with want,

Henry street overflowing with bodies
wanting a home, wanting a skyline to believe in.
And me, my own flesh delirious with rot,
bedridden for months at a time.

I yearned for punishment, an ending
that I could understand.
So I made a portal of my cunt for all
the hate we cannot name

and listened to the last breath of my spirit
leave my body.

Scatter-gun names you call me

Scanger

                                        Commoner

                        Cripple

                                Feeble-minded

                Scumbag

                                        Handicapped

Scrounger

                        Tramp

                                                Freeloader

        Lame

                        Knacker

                                        Waster

                Junkie

                                Retard

Dependant

                                                Schemie

                        Spastic

        Beggar

                                Mad

39

After

The truth is I was never used to this dread
until it came blistering between us,
an orchid blooming to death –
my body ripe with illness.

The truth is I never wanted any lover
to know the scent of sickness,
but you smell it, don't you?
The piss pot and my voice shaking
in my mouth again, the way my body
won't ever leave us to our lives.

Is it not enough to know
we won't ever have our own home?
I must hold it between my teeth
until it bleeds.

And some nights, when I can't even fuck,
I tell you I hate these fumbling organs.
You promise it's just for a season,
but the truth is I think I swallowed
the world.
I think I'm sick to death of it.

I wish you knew me before
I became what I am.
But then we wouldn't be us,
isn't that the lesson?

Doesn't there have to be a lesson?
Otherwise, what have we done
with all these years?

Otherwise, what do we do with this love?
Where does it go,
I mean, after?

I choose the living instead

On the day of the diagnosis
I go afterwards to the big church on Berkeley Road.
I don't believe in the god it was built for,
but I light a candle all the same,
try desperately to make the moment meaningful.

I don't try to stop myself thinking about desire,
the long wet quiet inside of me –

the things I dream about in silence;
a doctor with an answer and a way through.
My grandmother used to light candles
every morning for the dead.
I choose the living instead.

Outside, my mother is beside me
and soon there'll be tea in a flask
and the food my brother tendered with his hands.
Three bodies in the crisp of March
and the language between us is

thank god

please god

god bless.

All this god and not a Catholic in sight.
I choose the living instead.

You only care about animals and other men

You stand on Grafton Street with the usual sign –
meat is vicious murder.

> I should have known when the time ripened
> that you didn't know a thing about being hunted.

You talk about non-monogamy as if it's the saviour
of this rotting earth.

> I cut out my tenth rib with the kitchen knife,
> you salivate in your bedroom.

You beg me not to come home,
play your favourite songs on repeat.

> I go rabid in the winter-raw of Paris,
> bleed out tenderly for weeks.

You check for fingerprints in the bathroom,
call my living a crime scene.

> I vomit in your shower, forget how to sleep,
> consider again the implications of slow disease.

You send photos of defecation
to my phone, feed the tiny darkness.

> I lose the sound
> of my own voice inside my head.

You call me savage on my birthday,
then hang your triumph through the hallways.

What's real what's real what's real
I forget.

You tell it like a story, the slow
syndrome of my youth.

        I leave at midnight, take a taxi to the next
        sweet way out.

You wake in the morning still believing –
of course you were right all along.

        I wake in the hospital wet with dreaming,
        my heartbeat coming home.

Underlying condition

Language doesn't touch where it hurts
and I might long for you to be inside
this sentence but it's December
and the Taoiseach is speaking on the TV again.
Older now than we were that first time
in your parents living room,
after the birthday cake/before the ending,
but the same really, counting the dead,
saying things like *underlying condition,*
as if all these crooked bodies were to blame.

What counts as an underlying condition?
Cancer, diabetes, too old, too pregnant too young,
too strung out on the bus, too single mother,
too sick, too poor, too close to an ending, too
life-sparks-out-only-blackness-and-all-those-dreams-dead.
Is violence another rebirth?

You could never make it into this poem
if I hadn't killed you just a little,
(enough to know your mother still kisses me
on the forehead in my dreams most nights).
And winter will always be winter as long as
dead bodies light up the journey home.

I suppose memory will always be memory
as long as some of us forget,
(our quietly bruised lives rage on).
Everything changes and then nothing
at all and then the things I tell myself
long enough to wake up and live.

Post-mortem of the lives I left behind

On the first day of lonely,
my body is having one of its moments;
paralysis in any other country still maims the same.
I am not yet wilted;
                only addicted to the feeling of remembering.

There's still singing at the edges,
even if it's sirens, even if it's the wind going through
every memory I tried hard not to keep.
                All things need a grave in the end.

The sadness inside me has its own heartbeat.
Like how for years, I lamented a poorly insulated
flat on a hill behind the art college in Glasgow
                like it was the alter youth died on.

Tell me it's not a post mortem on the worst days;
that my mouth didn't taste like medicine for years.
My body is one street away from me.
                My voice is velvet somewhere.

Recovery

Not the word but the ending
we all must enter to finally understand
nothing lost ever really comes back again,
not like that.

I create the idea of it inside my head,
but in the end, it is just a room with
a limp body a long way from home.
A glimpse of light swelling through
window barely touches the feeling
of shutting down.

I've told you before,
but how to say it with words?
Again and again and again,
                  my heart stops.

Do you think that's a metaphor?
I lived it.
I felt the slow leaving of life.
I tried to warn the doctors,
tried to prove them wrong.
I stayed inside myself as everything ended
and what we call body
                  started again.

Body,
as lover

Crip love

for Aine

Before yet another panel about equality and inclusion you say
We can't have it all
It leaves me laughing for weeks, we don't have any of it, but I lied
Sometimes I can't sleep because there are too many things to love
You go for heart surgery on a Tuesday, not because you need
    any more opening,
I swear you've been all sky for years now
Disease does this to the bodies it misremembers for home
Everything that kills only wants to live
In June, I lie on your floor and marvel at the pink walls of your
    new house
But it's not enough, none of us are safe
I resent you bleeding every time another healthy person needs
    proof of the human condition
How many times will we die before –
but they've already forgotten, limp fruit in their summer plans
I go quietly none of the time
I'm trying to be honest, but it hurts
I tell you I've gotten my bladder movements down to four
    times an hour
You say that's not normal, but I'm just glad I've stopped pissing
    myself on the bus
I haven't killed anything in years
I saw a fox last night in the bins out back and it reminded me
    of our little kingdom
I cry every time I see a mother take the hand of their child, and
    you say,
I know

On the birth of your broken heart

you cook dinner for the first time in months
Roast squash and tomatoes, the delicate
pruning of flesh against flesh,
how every tender segment seems to want
for nothing at all
(desire becomes memory in the end)

You think about the butterflies at the beginning,
how slowly they bloomed into a fire alarm sick
with its own relentless ringing
And you haven't left each other yet,
but you can feel the ending in your mouth lately
(how he kisses it better but makes it worse)

After dinner, you lie on your stomach,
let your womb ripple open in its monthly release
The blood leaves your body and you think
how stale you've let these rituals become
(fear of his touch grows softly)

In the end it's just another knowing
that every boy becomes a man,
and that all life is frantic to fruit in the dark
(you made it out strong enough to bloom)

Nature poem (but make it bitter)

Lately every poem I read is beautiful and lying.
I don't trust your snow drops,

or the way you lose your grief in the blue.
It's too easy for you to make a poor body romantic,

make memory outside of the danger
of a missed meal or the way a heartbeat falters

to sounds outside the door at night.
It used to take us hours to reach the sea

from just a few kilometres away.
That's what I mean when I say love.

That's how hard we longed for the wide open.
And I'll tell you about joy in the spring,

how the earth unlocked every March,
at the first blooming of an ice cream siren,

and the games my mother played with us
on the slow bus to the mountains.

Everything we loved was beautiful and far away.
I resent you your freedom,

until I've known both worlds and still
I stay.

Parallel living

Say what you will about sound,
I know if I say the truth out loud
it'll keep ringing —
ricocheting on the south side of the city
near the mountains and small bodies of water.

I put your address into my phone,
watch a parallel life light up on screen.
I say I must be strange to think about your parents
in the quiet world of their tidy kitchen,
forget you a little less.

But what is grief if not the small things gone?
If not the back door opening onto your father's
garden, slow things blooming in January mist
and your sister's name starting in my spine
spreading towards sky.

I keep them secret, the things you did.
So secret that they'll never know why
I cut you so brutally from my living,
never returned to the scene of their love
even just to say goodbye with my voice

and not my life pruning in forward motion,
towards everything, towards anything at all.

Ode to the chamber pot

If you could, you might
choose to love what hurts, but I only ever
yearned for necessity. I choose to love the chamber pot
instead, Victorian darling of my body. Her round skin pale with
the balm of urine and years of quiet urgency. She waits under the bed
for the kiss of my longing to meet her wide wet lips. She misses the worst
years when I could hardly leave her. For a while, the day knocks against her as she
sleeps, but like all love stories history repeats, and I need her the same as my lost years.
Three am and I'm still pissing, hug of buttock inside her gaping mouth for hours.
The doctors try for a catheter, but they know nothing about her cradle,
how she pines for me in the hum of the night. She'd call it love,
this slow-burning need. I call her *mother* in my desperation
and promise to never leave.

Regression

We left the house at dawn.
My hair smelled of your shampoo
and I held in my throat all the ways
you made me scream the night before.
We kissed goodbye.

Later, I listened to the thing
inside my chest thump -
this isn't love,
this isn't love.

Symptoms of hurt (notes from my phone)

I called you a few weeks later, just to say I'd survived, as if you knew anything about it. By then we'd been separated for months, and I finally understood the difference between your temper and my self-preservation. Above all things, I understood that night in the bowels of your grandmothers old house, where you proved your past right. The way my voice went through your longing like it meant nothing at all. You said sorry later, of course, but the thing was already done, and I was tired of knowing that the men I love become the men I fear after all. But like most wounded creatures, I hungered for the moments before betrayal, when you were tender as a bruised beginning. And in my slow grief, I picked up the phone, begged you to say my name so that I could live another night believing

you were the answer.

Lullabies

I ate eggs today and felt terrible.
Like I'd locked the chickens in cages myself,
like I'd swallowed their dreams.
But it's not about the eggs, it never is.
It's not about the man who asked me to smile,
or how I've been sleeping too much lately,
exhausted and full of dreams too vivid
and too long.
I dreamt of all my past lovers last night.
Not one of us said sorry.

The gift

Did you save me that night in the water?
Not your body, because you never had one –
not a walking, breathing thing, but your spirit.

Did you whisper somewhere inside me?
I crawled out of my canal grave
and back into despair because I trusted it.

Were you waiting at the edge?
The thing that pulled me slipping up those tragic banks.
The phone ringing somewhere in the darkness.

Were you draped in a November sky?
The way I couldn't feel it in my body anymore:
the moon and her luminous language.
She was gone.
But you remained.
You pushed me out into the world once,
and I almost forgot your name.
Twin sister,
you've been missing
all these years.

Villanelle for the men I learned not to love

'Men are afraid that women will laugh at them.
Women are afraid that men will kill them'
—Margaret Atwood

I imagined my own annihilation after you left,
I loved your eyes most until the very end.
I swear I know my own dying best.

All the possibilities of murder kept me awake inside my head,
it was so much easier than the things you said.
I swear I know my own dying best.

I knew history repeating was your cruel caress,
on the day you called me crazy on the graveyard steps.
I swear I know my own dying best.

I dreamt of your rage deep into my chest.
The dead girls on the news kept me company when you left.
I swear I know my own dying best.

And even years later, when I learned you slaughtered afresh,
I bruised myself numb to survive that new death.
There were crows pecking at the lies inside your bed.
I swear I know my own dying best.

The goodbye notes

When I was twenty-eight and burrowed like a limp infant
on your double bed, you said nothing about growing up.

> Only fed me soup from the spoon and let the whale
> of my grief
> die every night in your aging arms.

The television hum, the screams on the street outside;
a lesson in how history dilutes – exhales – repeats.

> I won't say anything about rebirth,
> not here, not with language.

Only that my mind was broken for months but you held my sobs
like they were meant to dazzle and not drown.

> The night the police were called you held my hand in
> the sitting room,
> made sure they knew nothing would ever be taken
> from me that you could stop with your body.

I lied about the goodbye notes, but I can tell you now –
in my own long life:
I survived.

Body,
as protest

What I know by heart

Is this a sickness?
                        I woke with nothing to my name again
and all my memories of the future

gone dark.

The body is not a thing

'We as a society have to be prepared for 100,000–250,000
people dying each year from vulnerable groups, but for
everyone else, it will fizzle out'
—Dr. Peter Chin Hong

I play dead on a hotel room floor in Waterford,
because that's what I'm good at –
for years now.
The strange shackling of the chandelier above
my warped body, the palatial carpet on hived skin.
I warned my heart about places like this.
The luxury only frightens me because I am alien
to splendour.
I am bruised at the centre.
I was never everyone else.

I'm here because they care about accessibility.
I'm here because they must be seen to care.
I'm here because they want to love me.
One of these things is true.

Their language is my slow self-violation.
Twenty-five people died this week,
but the radio tells my mother the pandemic is over.

                              I cry on stage again.

It's a low soft hum,
the strength it took to stand   buckling.
Limbs greedy for the ground again,
the sweet home of the floor.
My heart has done this before.

A room full of strangers take their masks off
when I'm not around.
A summer day in May blisters with the sound
of all the people not here.

They care about sick lives.
They care about sick lives when I'm in the room.
They care about not being sick.

I take the money.
I go home early to a different room,
in the summer hum of the council estate
blue with my gathering heartbeat –
the largest luxury I know.

Testimony

I said your name in a Garda station
and the funeral inside my head only
    became less of a fiction.

I started screaming in my box room, the sound
    signalling out
        into the small night
            like a siren.

And just like in all the legends,
I was beautiful, but never free.

I confused your hands with
my lovers warmth and then buried us alive,
invited all your old friends to the wake,
as if that could save me,

Only later would I learn that survival
is what we leave behind in order to live:
    never our bodies,
but at least our rage,
    at least the beast inside our frames.

Every woman I know has imagined
    her own slow murder.

Think about that.

I want you to think about that
in the steady gloom of your night,
so that when you wake,
you'll finally be sorry.

I'm tired of being killed in my dreams.
I'm tired of your fingers
          inside
the wet ink of
          my body,
every time
          I'm forced to forget.

Sometimes, but rarely, I imagine
you out in the world,
think of who you could have been
if you hadn't left women like
                    slaughter houses,
I imagine you could have been beautiful,
but I hope
          you'll never be free.

An Irish goodbye

After a while I'm not sure I can call it love.
Sure, the night is familiar and humming.
The daily lullaby of hops on the wind
is heart-close and the Liffey will always be
the Liffey no matter what;
but I can't love what won't keep me.

It hurt years ago and then it got worse.
What do you call a wound that won't close?
No one can survive eight hundred euro a month
for a room with a gimp body for a bedframe
and a Pinterest page full of dreams.

The gulps of us the river swallows.
The diseases in my body that the state
refuses to name. What do you call a city
that becomes a wound?

I wish I could say something about the rain
on Capel Street or the rooms filled with
people I love waiting for the chimneys
on the shoreline to kiss the sky,
but that's all soul, and soul forgets itself
when it's not permitted to dream.

I tried to stay, over and over,
and every time, I grieve these streets,
knowing nothing beautiful can linger
in a landscape sick with want.
They made every heart a hotel instead.

Dublin, my love, you raised me to believe
and then you slaughtered me slowly.
Dublin, I only tried to save you
from another goodbye.

Forgiveness, and other freedoms

In the body, where everything must be honest,
I am ruthless in my shame.
I say   *forgive me*   and a sharp howl exits my lips.
I am still learning mercy.

I think of the body of my country, all the dead women I can name,
the doctors I can't afford to see because I'm poor and sick
and sick and –
which came first?

Who do I forgive at night?
You don't have to answer that.
You just have to promise me that you'll stay alive long enough
to puncture the night like it's your own freedom song.

Like it's your life growing old and not out,
and that everything – the world even –
belongs to you.

Love letter to my Tory nightmare

Did you kiss me in my sleep,
        and kill all my medicine?
I wake and watch the boys
on the road bruise slowly
with incarceration.
The brutal lives they can hardly
stomach hang –
            from their chapped lips.
I know you dreamed of this,
I know you put your lonely
where their mouths
are.
    You haven't written in weeks.
The soil is rotting black here.
The earth is a sick girl if I ever saw one,
the way you drill inside her,
        make her pale,
make her long for it.
I know you were lying when you told us
        we were safe.
Our loud lives are the first to
 scream.
I'd tell you I miss you, but you left me here
        alone.
I tend to my dying organs,
 you hand-cut   the poison,
salivate in your open-plan office,
then crawl
        home to your wife.
But I know you loved me first,
            deep
in that porn search on a Saturday night:

Teenage girl gets decimated
Working class slag scrounges hard
Darling, darling, construct my hurt,
then make it look like
love
 at the well-timed press conference.
You know, I killed you once,
 but it didn't last.
You only came back stronger.
I loved you once, but then
I remembered
                    I deserve to live.

How to kill a man and get away with it

Run like a girl,
after the club, after the spoiled offerings, inside the long night.

Punch like a girl,
into the slow gut of the world that raised you to be afraid.

Bleed like a girl,
once a month for years and years, curdle, writhe, rebuild.

Work like a girl,
twice as hard, for half the pay, just to live a little harder.

Fast like a girl,
cruel and emaciated and loved in all the wrong ways.

Die like a girl,
on the six o'clock news, at least once a week, knowing your
     killer so well.

Exhume like a girl,
unravel from the damp tarp of your dreams, unbury your
     viscous limbs.

Hunt like a girl,
find his day-job, file the teeth you have left.

Kill like a girl,
sharp, and wet, and scarlet – burn the evidence, eat him alive.

A moment to worship

In early Autumn you wonder again
what it is to love this body
from the outside in.
You lost the weekend
to the wreckage of yourself,

tried to call injection sites
    holy wounds
or some other altar,
but they kept bleeding
just the same.

You tried to find god in this body,
tried to love the judas of it.
And it's easiest on those summer nights
in Dublin when you can walk along
the coast and still breathe the same.

But the sea stays, even on the days
illness loosens for you to gasp through.
The truth is that you were never a tragedy.
Every time you dig yourself
above ground again
is a moment to worship.

I got better after you left

I don't mean the sickness quitting,
nothing as ordinary as that.
Madness came in winter of course.
Yes, Doctor, I'll take the pills.
No, Doctor, I haven't slept in months.
I can't disappear,
           the horror is within.

In January, another woman is murdered.
I go to the vigil alone, around the corner
from the office you sit inside each day,
lit up like a false god in the winter-dark,
and I remain hungry for an ending.

I used to tell you it hurt less when I lay
on my side, but the truth is you liked it better
when I flinched.
Yes, Sir, I am your slut
No, Sir, don't stop.
I am your –
limp fish to hook slowly.

All those years of playing dead
and still, we had dinner with your family.
Hung the delicate ornaments on the Christmas tree,
at night my mouth a holy portal for you to train.
Yes, Sir,
                the silence is within.
You begged me never to write about you.
My beloved, is this the trick?
I made my mouth the monster to siren
what remained, to salve the wounds

on my hands and knees,
to pry open the prison of your desire
just in time to never forget.

I know now when you say slut,
you still mean it.
Is this the trick?
I got better after you left,
it's that extraordinary.

Body,
as lighthouse

Begging for rain

My mother asks me to stop writing about
        darkness.
I go out to the garden,
bury myself in the dirt,
        beg for rain.

Life of the party

Every sickness gets better   or kills.
I am the strangeness in between.
You do not know where to put me,
I know,   I know,
you imagined my casket long ago.

I was lonely there too,
but beautiful enough for you to mourn
every summer that I cancelled plans
to lie in the dark of my own dull emaciation.

Love is the rooms I've given up in,
scattered across the flicker of the city
at night, and all I long for is the sweet
stir of my forgotten name.

I'm four years away from your mouth
the last time you said it out loud.
I'm four years deep into living in my
own hot piss.

You should have known   I'd conquer
the worst days alone.
Did you think you'd outsmart me?
I'm the queer darling of this show.
I've always been
                  the life of the party.

The Herbalist

He says every culture has another word for it:
the way we press our bodies against the ground
and ask the soil to sing.

I don't want to press my body against anything
that hurts anymore. I trust this man and his bare
feet more than the first doctor and the last.

I watch the soft spring of his body as he mixes
the tinctures, the slow potions that will gather
inside of me and then release.

The sea is waiting for me outside in its blue
salty gasps and the sky is birthing April
one sunrise at a time.

I pray the land I came from knows how hard
I long to stay.
When I'm leaving, he tells me there's no charge.

I keep this small tenderness inside of me for weeks:
the soft shiver of sea air,
the unassailing purr of new life.

December/I died trying

It's raining again
               and I'm holy,
not because I survived, but because
I died trying.

I only know I'm in the world
because wounds don't keep
                       dripping
from a body shuddered closed.

And I've been all wound this year,
playing fast in the dark with
      my
           own
                heartbeat.

Counting out the pills.
             Wading into the water.
Writing goodbye notes on my phone.
             I'm sorry I made the horizon go dark.

Later, in the emergency room,
they asked if I'd left a note.
I shook my head, turned my body
inside out until the day ended,
and I could leave behind what
I hadn't outlived.

Trust the damage

I forgot that things still grow in the night.
There's whole species under the sea
that light up in moonlight,
the soft glow guiding small creatures home.

We once thought that it was a sign
pointing to the edge of the world.
Nothing about god's kingdom,
just a dark ending to fall from.

I'm a small creature too, limping towards home.
The edge of my world had to come first:
the monster of my own sick blood,
I spent years not going easy.

Going savage in fact, going fatal,
until I came to surrender to the places
that this body takes me. I don't have to love
the days I can't crawl through or the nights

I wake paralysed.
I know I'll long for the next time
I'm lying on the kitchen floor waiting for the song
of yet another ambulance,

so that I don't have to
convince myself this was never meant to be.
I trust the damage.
Open the portal for the paramedics to arrive
into my emergency, and their night shift.
And as this ordinary rescue ripples,
I know I'll wake in the morning still sick,
but quietly baptised in the stars.

Elegy for all the years I stayed

You ruined me,
and I don't mean in a romantic way.

I mean you cut me into pieces
until I doubted my own freedom.

I think about your mother again,
her voice swells silken in the past.

I tried to make you the enemy,
but all I got were the things you said

to crack inside of me and live.
You were the victim of my sickness

just like everything else,
but the girl you said ruined your life

is in the papers again.
I never meant to follow her.

It's just she made such a beautiful villain
with all that truth.

All those years I called it love.
all those small cruelties could never be enough.

If I could reach your mother again,
I'd tell her only this:

I tried to save you from yourself.
I tried to forgive.

Everything deadly wants only to live

There are things you long for above all else:
an ending (any kind will do)
a cure (though you hate the way we're living)
your 30th birthday (only once)
a cure (the medicine will hurt)
your mother (over and over)
a cure (myth that is is)
a body that works on time (smell of urine and small dark)
a cure (leech out the dis-ease)
a hospital to hold you (too much to ask)
a cure (worn rag on the fairy tree)
a job you can keep (your body lurches)
a cure (though nothing bruised is not whole)
a home you can hold onto (Dublin haemorrhages futures)
a cure (everything deadly wants only to live)

The heartbeat on the other side of the headlines

Poor people triumph if only they work hard,
if only they wake at dawn and believe in a fair world.

I didn't get out.

I just learned how to not let the poor show.

I'm not the success story you tell yourself in the breach
of the night when you wake searching for a reason
to keep believing that the way we're living is right.

I couldn't see anything other than a *sick girl,*
tired girl/
scrounging off the state girl/
opposite of a dream girl/
dead girl on the news girl.
I let so much of everything die,
                    just so I could live.

This is what making it looks like:

the faces of my dead neighbours/
the dole queues on the way to infinity/
the survivor guilt at college graduation/
the spring flowers in my mother's garden/
the starlings murmuring through the estate
like they don't know a thing about organised abandonment
or dancing amongst burned-out cars.

I'm just the heartbeat on the other side of the headlines.
I'm just the story I will always try to save before the tragedy
of the grind kills every bright spark in the unshackled night.

My Precious Life

after Mary Oliver

It's winter again;
out in the world the bends in the road
turn sharper –
the trees go home for a while.
And the season lives inside my head too,
the last time I tried to return to the nothing
it was because I was so ripe for
endings, I forgot my own history.

The exquisite proof of it all,
that anything can stay living
and still be born again.
I once believed what lived in the nothing
could sustain me through the darkest days.
A wide-open absence to dream in,
a place for sickness to unfold its plume.

But what came next was forgiveness
and the stillness I found beyond the throbbing.
If I say it over and over, it will someday last –
my body, my body, my body,
sweet sister wreckage,
goddess of the get-through.
Nothing that bruises this bad ever lasts.

Yesterday was another day, and I stayed,
not because it stopped hurting,
but because if the sky tenders pink tonight,
and the birds hum their small bodies into flight,
then I promise,
I'll make something of my precious life.

THANKS & ACKNOWLEDGEMENTS

Going through a chronic and often life-threatening illness is a profoundly lonely and terrifying experience. My life and these words would not be what they are without the loving support of so many. To Carol and Tommie, thank you for raising me to believe in my future. To Carol, thank you for fighting for my life when I didn't have a voice. To Jamie, thank you for all the laughter and shared vision of a better world, we'll remember this for the rest of our lives. To Shannon, thank you for being there through all the heartbreaks, A&E visits, evictions, birthdays, knee-toppling laughter and triumphs. You're the love of my life. To Oran, thank you for the soul connection we share, for loving the sea the same as me, and for the staying alive pact. We've made it this far. To Lou, thank you for reading me poetry in bed, the late-night phone calls, and the not-so-creamy risotto. To Becca, thank you for coming into my life and cracking it open with your fierce love, compassion, and soul, and for the ways we can laugh. To Seánie, thank you for staying all these years, for always believing me, and letting me eat all your tofu. To Hazel, thank you for reading poetry with me on bookshop floors, for sitting with me in grief, for the voice messages full of singing, and your endless love. To Oisín, thank you for believing in a better world with me, for doing my food shopping during lockdowns and for the heartbreak car sessions on the M50. To Áine, thank you for showing me the meaning of community and for always being there, we can't have it all. To Jo, thank you for the spirit chats, heart connection and always, for the poems. To Chris, thank you for the love we share that as everything else changes, we hold onto. I hope it won't be too sweet. To Sophie, thank you for the Taylor Swift voice memos, the poems and this beautiful blooming friendship. To Chris Jude, thank you for the sanctuary of your beautiful home, the soul-nurturing conversations, and the kinship. To Michael, I've relearned what love really is with you, thank you for your heart. Here's to society collapsing. To Anne, thank you for loving me so fiercely and taking care of me, your home was always a sanctuary. To Niamh, thank you for your love and trust, and for letting me sleep in your bed for a week. To Phoenix, thank you for the love and always inspiring me that the revolution keeps going. To Niamh, Bee, David and everyone at Dublin Fringe, thank you for the endless support, chats and for the space for emergency poems. To Niamh, Elizabeth and Eoin at Poetry Ireland, thank you for your relentless support, and belief. To Pat and the team at Dedalus Press, thank you for believing in this book even in its earliest versions and for giving the manuscript so much care and attention. Thank you to my wonderful poetry teachers including Annemarie Ní Churreáin, Victoria Kennefick, Emmet Kirwan, Rebecca Tantony and Bridget Minamore. Thank you to the editors of the following publications and anthologies where some of these poems, or earlier versions of them appeared: *Poetry Ireland Review, Banshee, Poetry NI, Two Metre Review, Unapologetic Magazine* and *The 32: An Anthology of Working Class Voices*. To Arts and Disability Ireland, thank you for the financial support which made writing this book possible, and for all the invaluable support you give to disabled artists. To Jennie, Philip and Zoe, thank you for being my family for a while, you're always in my heart. To Annemarie, Mary, Marianne, and Jonathan, thank you for the space for healing and recovery, the support and loving kindness each of you have given me means the world. To A, you once made me promise to never write about you, you once promised you would never do it again to any other woman. I kept my promise as long as you kept yours. Finally, to the sickest versions of myself who dreamed of a way out, stay a little longer. I promise you make it.

www.ingramcontent.com/pod-product-compliance
Lightning Source LLC
Chambersburg PA
CBHW030501100426
42813CB00002B/299